TO

SPEAKING FROM THE SPIRITUAL DIMENSION

BY
GREG MAYHORN

Unless otherwise indicated, all Scripture quotations are taken from the *New King James Version* of the Bible.

Scripture quotations marked YLT are taken from the 1898 *Young's Literal Translation* by Robert Young.

Scripture quotations marked AMP are taken from *The Amplified Bible*. Old Testament copyright © 1965, 1987 by Zondervan Corporation, Grand Rapids, Michigan. New Testament copyright © 1958, 1987 by The Lockman Foundation, La Habra, California. Used by permission.

Tongues . . . Speaking from the Spiritual Dimension
ISBN: 978-1-939570-42-0
© 2014 by Greg Mayhorn

Published by Word and Spirit Publishing
P.O. Box 701403
Tulsa, Oklahoma 74170

Printed in the United States of America. All rights reserved under International Copyright Law. Contents and/or cover may not be reproduced in whole or in part in any form without the written consent of the Publisher.

ACKNOWLEDGEMENTS

I want to thank the following people for helping make this book a reality. Supernatural connections are so valuable to our lives.

First, to my wife, Glenna, who has been such a source of love, help, and encouragement to me for many years.

To my parents, Harland and Naomi Mayhorn, for training me to follow God from a young age.

To my secretary and sister, Tywanna Marcum, for her commitment to this vision and for her hours of work to help get this work published.

To my old friend, Gary Ball, whose years of experience as a newspaper editor was such an asset in transferring my original thoughts to a readable manuscript. Your time and effort are greatly appreciated.

And finally to the congregation of Freedom Word Church, who so faithfully receive me as their pastor. Thank you for allowing me this platform from which to minister!

CONTENTS

Preface vii

Chapter 1 – God's Secrets 1

Chapter 2 – Clarifying the Confusion 7

Chapter 3 – The Eternal Spiritual
Dimension 15

Chapter 4 – Spiritual Containers 21

Chapter 5 – Spiritual Communication 25

Chapter 6 – Receive What God Offers 31

Chapter 7 – Levels of Prayer 35

Chapter 8 – Practical Instructions 39

PREFACE

Of all God's Creation, only man has been given the ability to choose and speak words at will. This ability to communicate from our spirit sets us apart from all other created beings.

When God uses words, He creates, controls, and changes things. When we speak, we use words to produce the same results, albeit under the authority God gave us. We provide the "earthly" side of spoken words, and with that we operate on a level of authority far above all natural forces.

As Spirit-filled believers, we have the ability not only to speak with and from our understanding, but also directly from our spirit through the supernatural language of the Spirit—tongues. This is great news many know little about, but as you read on, you'll see just how powerful and profitable speaking in tongues really is.

One of the greatest heroes of the New Testament is the Apostle Paul. He probably did more to influence the Church over the last 2,000 years than anyone except for Jesus Himself. It was Paul who said in 1 Corinthians 14:18, *"I thank my God I speak with tongues more than you all."*

If you know anything about the Corinthian church, you know that means he spoke in tongues quite a bit. Though my experience isn't even close to the intensity and expertise of the great Apostle, I can say with him, "I thank my God I speak with tongues."

This book is about the vocal miracle called speaking in tongues, but because tongues—or language—is about communication, this is also a book about prayer, which is the most beneficial form of communication available.

PREFACE

Of all the benefits of the Spirit-filled life, it is the ability to pray in tongues that I value most. It has powerfully and eternally changed my life and ministry. If you'll use this great spiritual tool it will change your life too.

CHAPTER 1

GOD'S SECRETS

On a hot Wednesday evening in 2005, I went to the platform to minister in our mid-week service just as I had done for years. It's always exciting to stand before a congregation and bring a fresh and anointed word from God, but I had no idea what was about to happen. Little did I know we were about to experience something memorable and quite supernatural. We had no way of knowing that our nation's history was about to take a significant turn. Something was about to happen that would be a real surprise to many so-called experts.

I began to worship the Lord along with the congregation, as I often do in the beginning of my

TONGUES . . . SPEAKING FROM THE SPIRITUAL DIMENSION

ministry time, but the further we went, the more intense things became spiritually. We moved from just praise to intense prayer, and most of it was in the Spirit, or in other tongues. (See 1 Corinthians 14:14-15.) I prayed in the Spirit for a while along with the congregation, and then I began to hear myself speaking the interpretation of my prayer.

I kept saying the word "vacancy" over and over again. Then in a little while as I continued praying in tongues, I heard myself saying, "The right man for the job." I said this more than once also. We prayed a little while longer and the anointing to pray seemed to lift, so I taught my Bible lesson as planned. None of us knew what vacancy we were praying about, who the "right man" was or what "job" he was supposed to do.

I have learned over the years that we don't always know what we are praying about when we pray in tongues. God's secrets need to be prayed out, and praying in tongues is a way to get the job done without our mental reasoning and prejudices getting in the way.

If there is an interpretation, fine. If not, we are still effective because we are praying the perfect will of God when we pray in tongues. This is confirmed in Romans 8:26-27 where Paul points out that when the Holy Spirit uses us to make intercession, He does so according to the will of God.

When the service was over we went home and continued our week as usual, until on Friday the news reported a breaking story of national significance. Supreme Court Justice Sandra Day O'Connor surprised legal experts and court watchers by announcing her retirement effective when her replacement was confirmed.

This was the vacancy we had prayed about just two days before!

You can imagine how excited I was. Then it hit me—the other part of that interpretation said, "The right *man* for the job." I will admit this concerned me, because almost immediately the so-called experts began to wonder which woman President George W. Bush would appoint. The forces of political correctness were in high gear.

Justice O'Connor's historical position as the first woman to serve on the High Court, along with the fact she was the "swing" vote on the court—tipping the outcome on some very key issues, made her replacement all the more a politically important one.

It appeared another woman who was rather moderate in her views would, in all likelihood, be appointed. But thanks to our time of prayer in the Spirit, we had "inside information." Eventually, John Roberts was appointed and also named Chief Justice.

We obviously had "the right man for the job," according to the Holy Spirit.

One important note here is the fact that while many of us may not agree with Justice Roberts on every decision, we must keep in mind the disastrous results of having the "wrong" man for the job.

I am very much aware that we weren't the only ones who were praying at that critical season, but to think that God would and could use us to be a part of something that important is very exciting indeed. As a pastor responsible for ministering to the Body of Christ, I have to wonder how many of these opportunities are missed when we are just too busy, too carnal, or too uninformed to move in this dimension.

I am sure I have missed my share of them. But I've also been blessed to be involved with seeing the plan of God fulfilled in this earthly realm, and it's one of the most exciting and rewarding things in all the world.

One thing I am absolutely sure of is the fact that it was praying in tongues that placed us in a position to be used in such a powerful way. We must realize that powerful praying that shapes history is not relegated to the past or only for a select few Christian leaders. It is available today for those who will press into the eternal spiritual dimension and exercise authority through prayer and divine utterance.

Chapter 2

CLARIFYING THE CONFUSION

Before we go further, I think it would be wise to answer some questions about the use of tongues. Most of us realize that good and sincere people differ on the subject, but obviously somebody has to be right on the issue.

It's important to understand that we can be wrong in our head—or in our thinking—and still be right in our heart. However, it is impossible to exercise faith for a blessing we know nothing about. Therefore, it's very important to find the truth on this subject.

I was raised in a church that believed that people could—and sometimes do—speak in tongues, but that it was not really necessary. We were actually encouraged to stay away from the subject as well as those individuals who practiced speaking in tongues. There are, as you may know, some in the Church who actually believe it is of the devil and condemn speaking in tongues in any form. They believe there is no use for speaking in tongues today. These "cessationists" also don't believe that divine healing or prophetic ministry is available today. However, the problem with this position is that scripture doesn't support it.

The one scripture many cessationists use to support their position is 1 Corinthians 13:8 which says "tongues . . . will cease. . . ." However, this passage of scripture is referring to the future when we are in Heaven and won't need them. This scripture also goes on to speak of us no longer "knowing in part," which is another reference to the future.

CLARIFYING THE CONFUSION

Most honest observers and Bible students will admit we do not yet know all things and we still need the supernatural. Actually this generation—perhaps more than any other—needs to see the power of God in action.

On the other end of the spectrum there are those who seem to have no sense of order as to when and how tongues are to be used. In the name of freedom, these folks let things get out of order and sometimes bring more confusion to people than blessing. Some do not seem to know that there are different rules that govern these manifestations on both the public level and on the private side.

I have seen some pretty blatant abuses, but have come to realize that with proper teaching and spiritual leadership, people can be trained in the correct and beneficial use of this powerful spiritual manifestation.

Fortunately, the Apostle Paul spent a significant portion of the first epistle to the Corinthians giving instructions as to what these gifts are, and in particular, directions on the use of tongues in both public and private settings. (See 1 Corinthians chapters 12-14.) We are even told to "seek earnestly the spiritual things" (1 Corinthians 14:1 YLT).

It is in this portion of the New Testament that we see when tongues are used to address a group or a church congregation, there must be an interpretation given. Please note that it isn't a *translation,* but an interpretation. This gift of interpretation is only manifested as the Spirit leads, meaning we don't just choose to give a message in tongues at will. It is also important to note that God uses the available person regardless of their accent, educational level, etc. The gift is perfect, of course, but it is manifested through imperfect vessels.

The other use of tongues is the private, individual manifestation of a prayer language. It is given to us when we are baptized in the Holy Spirit, as we see numerous times in the book of Acts. It is a

CLARIFYING THE CONFUSION

supernatural ability given by the Holy Spirit, an actual vocal miracle to use for the rest of our lives.

One frequent question many sincere students have is, "Why?" While there are a number of reasons, I want to focus on two.

1. The ability to pray in tongues gives us the ability to bypass our mental limitations and reasoning faculties and pray directly from our spirit.
2. The ability to worship, sing, and praise in tongues is one of the ways we can worship "in spirit and truth" (John 4:23).

There are two things I want to point out about these characteristics of tongues. First, we can speak in tongues at will. Paul said in 1 Corinthians 14:15, "I will pray with the spirit, and I will also pray with the understanding." He was contrasting praying in tongues and praying in our known language, pointing out that we can choose to do either at will. When we are baptized in the Spirit

CHAPTER 3

THE ETERNAL SPIRITUAL DIMENSION

My earliest memories of church are being in small non-Pentecostal churches where people loved God, lived clean lives, and were looking forward to going to Heaven when their life here was over.

As a matter of fact, most of our singing and teaching had to do with the hereafter. We were very conscious of the realities of eternity to a degree. While we were well-acquainted with the idea of an "afterlife," we knew almost nothing about living in victory now. It seemed to us at least, that all the really good things were for later on, or in the words of one hymn: "When we all get to Heaven."

Our expectations for life here on earth were quite low. I'm sure there were a number of reasons why, but one of the biggest was the fact that we were not well-acquainted with the biblical concept of the "eternal spiritual dimension." Since we had little to no revelation about this truth, it is no surprise we had practically no understanding how our lives now are already involved with that realm, nor how blessed and powerful that connection can be.

What is the eternal spiritual dimension? While I don't pretend to have all the answers, I have learned some things about it that have changed my life greatly. For instance, I realize that eternity is not just a long time. It's actually outside the realm of time completely. People in Heaven don't ever grow old because there is no passage of time there. Eternity is a constant state of *now*. It's never

THE ETERNAL SPIRITUAL DIMENSION

yesterday, and nobody ever waits on tomorrow. It's always *now* in the spiritual dimension.

That's why faith is *now*. (See Hebrews 11:1.) A faith that is in the future is not really faith at all; it is, at best, hope. It's not possible to believe in the realm of tomorrow. We can only believe in the *now* based on what we are hearing *now* (see Romans 10:17) and faith is released by what we are saying *now*. That is what will change our tomorrows.

Another powerful aspect of the eternal spiritual dimension is the supernatural. It is above—or not subject to—the natural realm, or the laws that govern the natural world. When the power of that realm comes into this world, change occurs. The release of supernatural power is one of the threads woven into the fabric of scriptural history.

If you were to take the supernatural out of the Bible, you would have a common book no different or better than any other. However, when you realize the potential of the supernatural in the life of a believer, you come to the revelation Jesus gave us in Mark 9:23, which is ". . . all things are possible to him who believes."

There is nothing wrong in our lives that God's supernatural power cannot fix. This spiritual power is waiting to be released into this natural realm. As a matter of fact, releasing and using this power to bless humanity is one of our primary assignments as Christians.

It's also one of our greatest blessings.

You may be wondering what all this has to do with speaking in tongues. The truth is, the utterances given by the Spirit in this way are right out of the eternal spiritual dimension. They are not natural, but supernatural.

Speaking in tongues is one of the primary ways to tap into this powerful realm of the Spirit. It is a key to "walking in the Sprit." (See Galatians 5:25.) It is one of the most spiritual activities we can engage in, opening the door for the supernatural to invade our world.

If I were the devil, I would want to confuse, divide, and generally misinform the Body of Christ about this biblical truth. I would seek to make it an issue that people would choose to ignore. However, one of the things I have learned is that those things Satan fears are the things most important to God and to my success as a believer. Of all that being "Spirit-filled" means, it is the ability to speak in a supernatural language that I prize the most and have found to be the most effective benefit of being baptized in the Holy Spirit.

Chapter 4

SPIRITUAL CONTAINERS

It has been said that words are like containers. They hold life or death, blessing or cursing. (See Proverbs 18:21.) Jesus taught us that by our words we are either acquitted (or justified), or sentenced to punishment (condemned). (See Matthew 12:37.)

Words can literally change the atmosphere of a room whether 2 or 2,000 people are present. These unseen, yet very real, spiritual containers are powerful whether they are positive or negative. It's really quite astounding that God would allow man to operate on this level of authority and have the ability to release such power at will, but it is so.

This level of authority and partnership with God can only be understood through revelation of the Word by the Holy Spirit, which is available to us for the asking. (See Ephesians 1:15-23.)

The order of blessing goes like this: God speaks, we hear, we process (meditate on and receive the revelation), we believe, and then we speak. (See Romans 10:17; Joshua 1:8; Mark 11:22-24.) The positive power of words is so important to God that not only did He use them to create the world in the beginning, but He made sure that words of blessing were the first words Adam heard. (See Genesis 1-2.) When the Apostle Paul spoke of this in 2 Corinthians 4:13, he actually quoted from Psalm 116:10 when he said, "And since we have the same spirit of faith, according to what is written, 'I believed and therefore I spoke,' we also believe and therefore speak." The Spirit of faith is

SPIRITUAL CONTAINERS

always obvious. It is revealed through the words we choose to speak and our corresponding actions. (See James 2:20-26.)

The curse works the same way, but in the opposite direction. The devil speaks, people hear, then process, believe, and speak. Over time these negative and destructive words come to pass in the lives of those who constantly speak them.

It is sad that so many people are cursing their lives every day with their own mouth and are not even aware of it. Their words are condemning them to lives far below what God wants them to have. It is a life planned for them by Satan, and even though they don't realize it, they are constantly reinforcing it with their own mouth.

The choice really is ours, not God's. From the beginning He gave us the authority to choose and speak words, and as each of us choose daily what comes out of our mouths, we are either blessing our lives or cursing them.

CHAPTER 5

SPIRITUAL COMMUNICATION

When we speak, our voice provides a connection between this present temporal (temporary or subject to change) world and the eternal (fixed or unchanging) dimension. The natural, material realm is tied to the spiritual one through the power of words, or we could say through communication on a spiritual level. While words of faith and scriptural accuracy go into both the seen and unseen realms, it is the speaking with other tongues that takes us beyond our own soulish ideas and thinking. Tongues do not come from our head, but from our spirit. This eliminates the possibility of human reasoning and emotions tainting our communication with God.

Some have the idea that since God knows everything, it doesn't really matter how we pray. His Word, however, shows us otherwise. Jesus Himself gave us much precise teaching on the subject of prayer because it must be done correctly in order to receive an answer.

Let me give you another example of the power of praying in other tongues. As a pastor, I obviously want our church to grow. I use my faith for people to come—both those who need to be with us and those who are needed to help fulfill the vision. I pray about this with my understanding, using my faith to believe for growth. I am sure this is effective, but I also have learned that there is a deeper dimension of prayer even in this area.

Let me explain.

We have a Monday night Prayer School that meets for teaching about prayer and to spend time

SPIRITUAL COMMUNICATION

praying together, particularly for things concerning the vision and ministry of our local church body and for requests that come in to us.

One night a few years ago we were in a time of corporate prayer. In other words, everyone was praying aloud at the same time. Let me say that I'm not against one person praying and the group agreeing with the prayer, but that's not the only way to pray. We must be careful not to get so caught up in our religious traditions and habits that we miss out on all the good things God has for us.

Maybe you are not used to everyone praying at once, or even praying out loud, but don't be alarmed. It's scriptural. Besides that, God is the only person in the universe that has the ability to clearly hear each and every one of us at the same time with perfect understanding of what's being said. It is so worth the effort to learn to flow with the move of the Spirit in a given situation and enjoy the blessings of God.

TONGUES . . . SPEAKING FROM THE SPIRITUAL DIMENSION

On this particular Monday night I began praying, and as is often the case, I soon began to pray in other tongues. As I did, I began to get a word in my spirit; a type of word I have learned needs to be spoken out.

It was an English word that was a word of interpretation to what I was praying about in tongues. It was rather strange for me as the word was "Chesterfield." It certainly wasn't something that came from my head.

As a child of the 50s and 60s, I was familiar with the old Chesterfield brand of cigarettes, but obviously God wasn't having me pray about that. I didn't know what I was praying about, but I sensed the presence of God upon the matter and prayed it out more, speaking the word a number of times.

Sometimes it is necessary to speak something like this over and over. For some reason, the release of faith and authority needs to be emphasized stronger than normal. Whatever the reason, I have learned to follow the Holy Spirit and stay with something like this until I sense He is finished, at least for the time being.

Since others were nearby, I tried to restrain myself from speaking too loudly as I did not want to draw attention to this strange word in prayer. An important note here is that if I was not in a prayer meeting where people understood these things, it would have been better for me to have excused myself to do this privately. It's important to keep what we do in proper order and protocol.

The service ended and we went home. I told no one about this and waited. Actually, I forgot about it somewhat until about two weeks later when a wonderful family attended our church for the first time at a Sunday morning service. One of things so interesting about them was they had four pretty little girls who were like stair steps, in size and age. They were excited about the service and I just could tell something was "special" about this relationship we were beginning.

After the service I met with our praise team for lunch. Our team leader was a school teacher and as we mentioned this new family, she said she knew them and taught one of the girls in her class. She also mentioned they were from . . . you guessed it, "Chesterfield," which is an area outside Richmond, Virginia.

I realized this was the family I had been praying for. They were new to the area and needed a good church. They have since become an active part of the ministry, and both they and the church have been blessed by the connection. Of course there was no way I could know this, but the Holy Spirit did! Oh, thank God for the wonderful ability to pray out the will of God through the power of spiritual language.

Chapter 6

RECEIVE WHAT GOD OFFERS

Obviously, the whole experience of speaking and praying in tongues is connected to the Pentecostal blessing poured out on believers. It first began in the upper room and has continued to this day.

This baptism in the Holy Spirit is not a temporary blessing or something only needed to empower believers of the past. On the contrary, if ever there was a time in human history when the Church needed the supernatural abilities of God it's now, in the perilous times of the end.

So the first practical concept is that of acceptance—saying yes to God's plan and purpose of which tongues is a part. I'm amazed at how many Christians think they are sold out to God until He presents them with something they have not been accustomed to in their religious past. Some seem to think the Kingdom of God is like a buffet. We just go along and choose what we want according to our tastes.

I am quite direct on this issue because I've been there. Speaking in tongues was not one of the things I was interested in for the first five years or so of my Christian life. I was pretty much "anti" tongues and wasn't eager to pursue them. However, when I was presented with the Spirit's fullness as a 15-year-old teenager, I reached out to God with an honest heart and He met me with a new dimension of His presence. Jesus baptized me in the Holy Spirit. (See Mark 1:8.)

I began to speak in tongues just like those early believers did on the day of Pentecost. It wasn't a fluent, diverse stream, instead just a trickle that has since grown to a river of supernatural communication that is one of the most valuable spiritual activities I engage in. However, I would not enjoy this wonderful blessing today had I not accepted what God offered to start me on this spiritual journey.

Once we are convinced of and accept the truth of God's will for us to be baptized in the Spirit and speak in tongues, we need to receive that fullness. It is like any other blessing offered by our Father. We just simply receive by faith what He makes available. This means prayer is a great way to receive. Just ask and believe you receive. (See Mark 11:24.)

If you truly receive by faith, you can then expect to have "utterance" in your spirit or inner man. It's that utterance, or urge to speak, that we need to release through our tongue or voice. It won't be your native language, so it will sound strange to your ears. It is a way for God to bypass our mental and reasoning faculties to allow us to pray directly from our spirit.

Don't make the mistake of thinking the Holy Spirit is going to speak for you. He doesn't speak in tongues—we do! Look again at Acts 2:4. It tells us "they . . . began to speak" in tongues. The Holy Spirit isn't going to force or drive us to speak, either. That's how the devil operates.

No, the Holy Spirit is a perfect gentleman, so to speak. Paul said "I will pray with the spirit" (1 Corinthians 14:15). We can choose to yield to the Spirit and speak, or we can choose not to do so.

Once we begin to speak, the next step is to keep on doing it. Don't stop at the door, but go on into this new room of spiritual things. It will revolutionize your prayer life, and open the door to the deeper things of God.

CHAPTER 7

LEVELS OF PRAYER

One of the things we learn as we study and practice prayer is that it is done on various levels. Many of us don't pray today on the same level that we did when we were first saved. We have grown and should continue to do so.

There are different levels and types of prayers that accompany different levels and types of spiritual development and ministry. Regardless of where we are now, you can be sure God doesn't want us to stay at this place. There is a greater level of effectiveness and power that we can attain.

A wonderful benefit of moving higher in our prayer level is that we will enjoy a greater level of the supernatural here on Earth. Our blessing level will increase. Often, people think they need to work harder or longer, or they need more education, or perhaps to know certain people to receive more of God's blessings. However, the truth is many probably just need a more productive prayer life.

There is the most basic of levels where we pray about our needs and those whom we love; where our prayer life is consumed with "me." We've all been there. That is where we started—but that's not where God wants us to stay.

One of the things we need to grasp is balance. Successful and powerful prayer is a balance between:

- Prayer we initiate, and prayer God initiates;
- Prayer for ourselves, and prayer for others;
- Prayer for material things, and prayer for spiritual things;
- Prayer to change things, and prayer to change us;

LEVELS OF PRAYER

- Prayer in our known language, or our "understanding," and praying in tongues.

Achieving balance in these areas comes with time and experience in prayer. We don't arrive overnight, but we should be continually growing. To do this, we must constantly be learning about this great subject. We learn by doctrinal teaching, through mentors who show us by example, and by experience—by doing it ourselves. We should always be learning and growing in our prayer life.

If you sense you are stuck at a level and don't know exactly how to get to the next one, go back to these three basic areas.

1. **Are you still being taught to pray?** In Luke 11:1, one of Jesus' disciples asked Him, "Lord, teach us to pray. . . ." Jesus began immediately to do so. It can be learned.

2. **Do you have prayer mentors who are at a higher level who can inspire you?** It's important to not be intimidated by those

who know God better than we do, but to be inspired by them.

3. **Are you spending regular quality time in God's presence?** Nobody ever became a great cook or a good driver by just reading about it or watching a video. They didn't even get there by just being with someone who already was good at it. They had to "do it!"

In all the areas of balance we looked at, praying in tongues is a great help because it allows us to follow the perfect will of God and tap into the mind of the Spirit. This, in turn, helps us avoid selfishness and limited focus. No matter how smart we may be, we just don't know all we need to know to cover all these areas accurately and effectively. We need the Spirit's help in prayer, and speaking in tongues is one of the greatest helps He offers.

Chapter 8

PRACTICAL INSTRUCTIONS

Speaking in tongues on any level is supernatural. It's not just a mental or physical exercise, though obviously we are aware we're doing it and it does involve the physical aspect of using our vocal abilities.

This means we must learn to cooperate with the utterance given deep within our spirit by the Holy Spirit. We have to learn to connect our tongue with our heart and let the river flow. (See John 7:37-38.) How is this done? In these many years of using and enjoying this supernatural gift, I've learned some valuable lessons that I want to pass along to you.

First you must "speak" or actually enunciate the sounds, syllables, and words that come up from your spirit or inner man. You cannot speak effectively and fully without moving your lips and tongue. I realize this sounds so elementary that it borders on the ridiculous, but you can't speak fluently if you don't speak fully.

Don't just whisper or mumble. Obviously there are times when we must pray softly, but sometimes it is necessary to get louder. It may be necessary to get alone somewhere so you aren't concerned about someone hearing you. Then, just throw caution to the wind and pray from your heart. Remember, the Holy Spirit always has our best interest at heart and will never lead us wrongly.

Notice in Acts 2:4 that the people on the day of Pentecost "began" to speak. This was a beginning, not the end. In the natural realm, when children

PRACTICAL INSTRUCTIONS

learn to talk, they are very limited in their vocabulary. The same is usually true of our spiritual language as well. Let me point out here that a person might have been saved a long time and be a stalwart Christian in many ways. However, if they are new to the Pentecostal experience they are "babes" in this area. It will take time for them to become fluent in the language of the Spirit, but if they will stay with it, this language will grow and their effectiveness in prayer will increase.

Have you ever talked to someone who hardly moved their mouth? It's pretty odd and certainly affects the way they speak. This is true in the area of speaking in tongues as well. Just throw caution to the wind and let it out. It does not always have to be loud to be effective, but it has to be adequately enunciated or spoken.

Secondly, we must learn to get our head out of the way. Our emotions and reasoning can keep us from the deeper flow of the Holy Spirit. When we allow this to happen in prayer, we won't speak on that deeper level God wants to take us into, and it is this deeper level that will produce the results we need and want.

Learning to quiet the mind is so valuable, but it's a discipline that takes time to learn. Praying in tongues is a good way to get to the place where, instead of our intellectual reasoning dominating our thoughts, the Holy Spirit can relate the mind of God to us. (See John 16:13-15.)

The third key I want to share with you is to pray long enough to break over into the deeper realms of God. In James 5:16 (AMP) it is described as "making tremendous power available." This kind of praying is intense. It's not done while our minds are occupied with other things. Although I like to pray in tongues while doing other things, this type of prayer is focused. It means doing nothing else but focusing on prayer and continuing to do so until you break through.

PRACTICAL INSTRUCTIONS

Sometimes it is easier and quicker than at other times, but I've found that if I will pray long enough in tongues, I will eventually get there, and getting to that place is so needed and so beneficial. Things will be revealed that we would not otherwise know. Things will be prayed out that otherwise would not be, and things will happen that would not otherwise happen.

John Wesley said, "It seems God is limited by our prayer life. He can do nothing for humanity unless someone asks Him." I am convinced that there are things that will never happen—even though they are God's will—unless someone prays on this deeper level. This deeper level almost always involves praying in tongues, and usually involves a protracted time of such prayer.

There are no shortcuts. If we are to have the results we see in those mightily used by God, we will have to follow the same path they traveled—the pathway of fervent prayer.

TONGUES . . . SPEAKING FROM THE SPIRITUAL DIMENSION

Let me share one of those "fervent" times of prayer from my own experience. Some years ago I was awakened in the early hours of the morning with a burden of prayer. I could sense the Holy Spirit stirring me.

As I yielded to that leading, it grew to the point that I got up and continued praying. I could sense an urgency and intensity that compelled me to press into a deeper level of prayer in the Spirit. I prayed for quite a while in tongues with enough volume that my wife could hear me even though I was praying in another room. I continued on until I felt a "release" in my spirit. I knew I had made progress and my prayer had made a difference.

But for what or whom I did not know.

The next morning a phone call came about a family member in the emergency room with some very ominous symptoms, some of which, in my years as a pastor, I had seen in people with terminal conditions.

PRACTICAL INSTRUCTIONS

It did not look good in the natural, but thank God for the Holy Ghost who had already dealt with the situation the night before as I prayed!

Everything turned out okay and that person is still alive today, and hasn't had that problem since.

Some might say that it was coincidence, or that the individual would have been fine anyway. There's always someone trying to explain away the supernatural. You may as well get used to that. But what are the chances that all of these circumstances came together by accident? I was not aware this individual was sick, and believe me, I hardly ever awaken at that hour of the night for any reason.

Besides this, I know the Holy Spirit. We have a working relationship and I recognize his "tug" on my heart. No one can convince me that God did not use praying in tongues to break through the problem and move that situation to one of victory.

It is important to understand that this type of experience is not reserved for or limited to preachers or those who have been saved many years. It's available to all of us and it should actually be something we all become familiar with.

The fourth area of practical instruction is to believe for interpretation of our tongues as the Spirit wills. Since interpretation of tongues is a spiritual gift, as well as the tongues themselves, it is subject to the will and direction of the Spirit of God. (See 1 Corinthians 12:11.)

Many times while praying in tongues, I'll get a word or a phrase that is in English but realize it's not from my head—it's from my spirit. I know it is something that needs to be spoken out. It is an interpretation of that which is being spoken in the Spirit.

I shared an example of this in Chapter 1, when we were praying on a Wednesday evening several years ago and I spoke the word "vacancy," only

PRACTICAL INSTRUCTIONS

to learn two days later a vacancy was occurring on the Supreme Court. I kept saying that one word "vacancy" over and over until I felt a release to move on. Then the phrase, "the right man for the job" began to come. I didn't understand what we were praying about, but I knew we were in a vein, so to speak, and that speaking out these things was needed. Sometimes it's a word and sometimes just a phrase, but it is important. I knew I was led to do this—not just that time, but many other times as well. For a long time I didn't understand why.

Why would it be necessary to say something over and over? After meditating and reflecting on scriptural principles, I've come to what I believe is a powerful conclusion. When we speak out these words and phrases of interpretation for what we have prayed in tongues, we are releasing faith and authority. These are two spiritual forces necessary to change things in this natural realm.

We are in essence releasing the thing we are praying about into this earthly realm. We are cooperating and working with God to see His will and plan accomplished here on earth as it is in Heaven.

Oh what a privilege!

ABOUT THE AUTHOR

Greg Mayhorn was born and raised in the coalfields of Appalachia. Born again at age 10 and filled with the Holy Spirit at 15, it was while working as an underground coal miner and also serving as a pastor that he answered the call to full time ministry in July 1980.

While pastoring a small Pentecostal church in the early 1980's, he first became acquainted with the message of faith and the great teaching revival of that era. For 30 years now he has faithfully ministered the full gospel faith message through various avenues at different times including: church services, radio, television, and the printed page.

Taking what are sometimes complicated biblical doctrines and questions and making them easy to be understood is a characteristic of the ministry God has given him to fulfill. With an emphasis on the integrity of God's word, the anointing, gifts of the Spirit and divine healing, his ministry has touched many lives over these last 30 years.

Greg and his boyhood sweetheart Glenna have been married for 39 years. They have two children and six grandchildren. They make their home in Lynchburg, VA, where he has pastored Freedom Word Church in nearby Appomattox for the last 23 years.